THE TWELVE
O'CLOCK COOKIES

DURANDA LEWIS-MARCHELL

DEDICATED TO GOD OUR CREATOR, THE DAISY OF
EL CALLEJON AND ALL THE BEAUTIFUL PEOPLE
OF EL CALLEJON

WRITTEN BY DURANDA LEWIS-MARCHELL

ILLUSTRATED BY ABBI MURILLO

KD Publishing

This is El Callejon, a small community in the mountains of the Dominican Republic.
The community is full of beautiful children.

There is a safe place in the community where children come and go. They always look for the Daisy of El Callejon. "Daisy, Daisy!" They call as they go by the safe place. The Daisy of El Callejon runs to the door waves and smiles at the children.

One day at twelve o'clock a little boy named Edison stopped by to talk to the Daisy of El Callejon about his dream of being a fireman but she could tell he was very hungry so she gave him cookies.

Cookie, cookie, twelve o'clock cookie,
visit each and every day.
Cookie, cookie, twelve o'clock cookie,
"Please fill my tummy," I say.

Edison stopped by day after day exactly at twelve o'clock. One day, after his sweet time in the safe place, as he was walking home, he saw his friend, Yafreisi.

Smiling, he told her all about the yummy cookies he ate with the Daisy of El Callejon.

The very next day, Yafreisi went with Edison to talk with the Daisy of El Callejon to see if she could get a cookie, too. Of course, the Daisy of El Callejon smiled and gave them both cookies.

Cookies, cookies, twelve o'clock cookies,
now, two visit every day.
Cookies, cookies, twelve o'clock cookies,
"Please fill our tummies," we say.

Edison and Yafreisi walk down the dirt road to school every morning. They can't wait until twelve o'lock when they get to stop at the safe place to talk with the Daisy of El Callejon and eat yummy cookies. They love eating cookies almost as much as they love the Daisy of El Callejon.

Cookies, cookies, twelve o'clock cookies,
now, two visit every day.
Cookies, cookies, twelve o'clock cookies,
"Please fill our tummies," we say.

One day, another friend, Endry, overheard Edison and Yafreisi talking about the safe place and wished he could go with them.

Edison and Yafreisi invited their friend to be a part of the twelve o' clock cookies.

That very day, at twelve o'clock, the three amigos ran to the safe place. When they ran through the door, the Daisy of El Callejon smiled because she knew what they wanted. She went to the cupboard and took out enough cookies for all three amigos.

Cookies, cookies, twelve o'clock cookies,
now three visit every day.
Cookies, cookies, twelve o'clock cookies,
"Please fill our tummies," we say.

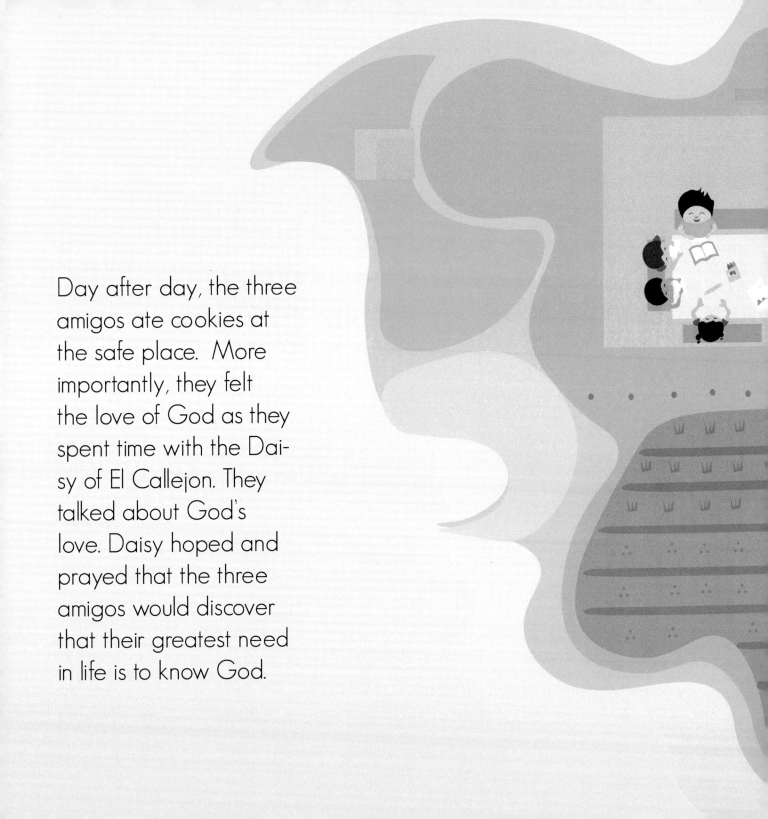

Day after day, the three amigos ate cookies at the safe place. More importantly, they felt the love of God as they spent time with the Daisy of El Callejon. They talked about God's love. Daisy hoped and prayed that the three amigos would discover that their greatest need in life is to know God.

Cookies, cookies, twelve o'clock cookies,
now three visit every day.
Cookies, cookies, twelve o'clock cookies,
knowing God is the only way.

The twelve o' clock cookies grew to love and know God. They will always remember the love they received at the safe place and will always remember the love of God shown to them in the form of a cookie.

Cookies, cookies, twelve o'clock cookies,
pass on God's love today.
Cookies, cookies, twelve o'clock cookies,
knowing God is the only way.

68552629R00015

Made in the USA
Middletown, DE
21 September 2019